Free-Range Writing: 75 Forays For The Wild Writer's Soul

First published in 2017 by Five Lanes Press

Contact: info@fivelanespress.com

Contact: author@jennyalexander.co.uk
Website: www.jennyalexander.co.uk

ISBN:	Paperback	978-1-910300-22-0
	ebook	978-1-910300-23-7

Cover: Rachel Lawston http://lawstondesign.com
Interior: Zebedee Design

FREE-RANGE WRITING

75 FORAYS FOR THE WILD WRITER'S SOUL

JENNY ALEXANDER

five lanes

Contents

Why free-range writing?

Many writers start out with an idea of what kind of thing they want to write and then never stray from that area of writing. That's a shame, because thinking of yourself as just a novelist, or a poet, or a memoirist, or a non-fiction writer means you don't get to explore the full range of your writer self.

Free-range writing means spreading your creative wings and experimenting with new ways of expressing yourself through short forays into different areas of writing.

This is hugely energising for your creative spirit – creativity is, after all, about trying new things or doing familiar things in new ways. It will also help you bring fresh ideas and skills back to your chosen area of writing:

- If you normally write fiction, writing some poetry can help you develop a more lyrical prose style, and raise your awareness of the power of imagery; writing non-fiction and memoir can help you notice the breadth of knowledge and experience you can bring from your own life to your fictional settings and situations.

- If you're primarily a poet, doing some fiction and memoir writing can help you develop narrative, character and conflict, and think about point-of-view; writing non-fiction can extend your range of themes and subjects.

- If you're a memoirist, writing fiction can help you find the compelling story among the mass of remembered events and details; writing poetry can help you express the emotional power of your experiences, and writing non-fiction can help you anchor your story in its historical, cultural and geographical context.

- If you're a non-fiction writer, one issue is how to engage your reader. Writing fiction, poetry and memoir will help you find a narrative voice and focus that draws readers in and holds their interest.

As well as boosting your skills in your normal area of writing, free ranging can open up whole new avenues you may not have considered exploring before. For example, in my recent memoir writing workshops, one of the participants discovered she loved writing poetry. Having felt daunted by the idea of writing a prose memoir, she was keen to experiment with writing about her early life through a collection of poems.

In other courses, writers who had only ever considered writing stories have been surprised how much they enjoy writing non-fiction, and several have had articles published in magazines, alongside their normal fiction writing.

There's no reason why anyone should stick to one writing identity, and free-range writing will help you break out and think of yourself as a writer, rather than just a novelist or a poet, a non-fiction author or a memoirist.

When you think of yourself as a writer, everything is inspiration: your memories of the past, your knowledge and experience, your physical environments, your fantasies and feelings, your insights and the symbols that create your personal connections to the world.

So free-range writing doesn't only expand your sense of yourself as a writer; it expands your awareness of yourself as a person, and makes your whole life feel richer and more resonant.

Venturing forth

There are seventy-five writing tasks in this book and they'll take you in all sorts of different directions. Every fifth one offers a choice of genres on a theme – and that brings the possible total to well over a hundred fantastic forays.

It isn't a course. In fact, it's the opposite of a course. There are no learning goals and assessments. So how will you know that it's helping to make your writing better?

Goals and assessments are linear; they keep you on one single track. Free ranging is open and organic. You'll know you're succeeding when you notice you aren't even thinking in terms of writing better.

You don't need to think in terms of writing better because you'll feel it happening automatically the more you explore your writing possibilities. You'll find yourself moving more strongly and confidently into your own voice.

When you set off on your writing forays, attitude is everything. Think of each one as an adventure, and approach it in a playful way. You aren't trying to write well; you're trying to find out what's moving in your mind, capture it on the page, and see how it feels to be writing off your normal track.

Learning through play

In her book, *Becoming a Writer*, Dorothea Brande talks about the writer as needing to recognise and nurture two separate selves, which she characterises as the rational grown-up and the playful child.

Free-range writing is learning through play, the way small children learn. It's learning through doing, rather than receiving abstract information and instructions.

The toddler in the bath will pour water from one container to another, time and time again. She will watch what happens to the stream of water when she tips it slowly and tips it fast. She will be fascinated by the way it adapts its shape to different containers, how it moves over objects and how it feels when it falls on her skin.

No one tries to explain the particular properties of liquids and solids to a little child, because the best way for her to learn is through experimenting, and that is the best way for writers to find their voice.

Some people struggle to believe that playing is productive; to them, it feels like wasting time. Perhaps that's partly because playing is pleasurable, and we prefer to think achievement comes only from hard work.

But pleasure is the key to writing success. If you enjoy writing, you'll do more of it, and if you do more, you'll gain in confidence, skills and awareness. As your feelings of competence grow, you'll enjoy it even more, and so the happy cycle goes on.

Therefore it's important to nurture your ability to be playful and come to your free-range forays, as Brenda Ueland recommends in *If You Want to Write*, 'like a child in kindergarten, happily stringing beads.'

<u>Tips and directions</u>

Because some areas of writing may be unfamiliar to you, the tasks are more than just prompts; they include some tips and directions.

If you feel you'd like a bit more guidance, there are some general pointers on writing stories and memoir at the back of the book, and also some notes on non-fiction and poetry.

These are at the back because, unlike traditional writing courses, free-range writing doesn't start with theory and follow with practice; it starts with writing, and your understanding of the way it works grows naturally from that.

Like everything else in this book, you can choose at what stage you want to read my notes, or indeed whether to bother with them at all!

The only rule

Most of the tasks have a suggested time limit, and it's really important to try and stick to it. Short, timed pieces mean you have to dive in and just write whatever comes, without too much pondering. Your inner critic hates them!

When you don't have time to over-think, you have to write instinctively, and one of the things you can learn from writing instinctively is that you can trust your instincts.

Another great learning from just getting on with it is that you don't have to sit around waiting for inspiration; you can write any time you decide to make space for it, and on pretty much any topic.

The many possibilities

There are lots of ways of incorporating some free ranging in your writing life, and how you do it will depend upon what you want to get from it and what kind of person you are.

Here are some possibilities:

- Make one little foray a day. A short burst of writing every day is a tried and tested method for getting things flowing again if your writing feels stalled. It's the main idea in some of the most loved books for writers, including Dorothea Brande's *On Becoming a Writer* and Julia Cameron's *The Artist's Way*, and many writers swear by it.

- Make one or more forays as and when the fancy takes you. This is to a daily practice what a notepad is to a page-a-day diary. If you aren't keen on regular commitments, or your lifestyle at the moment makes it difficult, you can make a few free-range forays now and then to pep things up when you want to get some fresh perspectives and ideas.

- Gorge yourself on free-range writing binges, the way you might get stuck into a box set instead of pacing yourself between episodes on TV.

- Mix it up! Do one a day for a couple of weeks, then take a break, have an occasional flurry or a box set binge and then go back to one a day.

Within each one of those approaches, there are even more possibilities. You could

- Do the seventy-five forays in the order they're given, not skipping any.

- Take potluck, doing whichever ones the book falls open at.

- Flick through and choose ones you particularly fancy doing – but do be aware that the ones that don't appeal may be the ones that could surprise you.

- Revisit them more than once. Many of the tasks begin with writing a list of topics so, having chosen one to write about, you could do the task again, choosing another.

- Adapt them. You can always take a task and create your own variations.

Whichever way you decide to tackle the tasks, you'll find a handy tick list at the back of the book, so you'll be able to see at a glance which ones you've done.

Finally, you don't have to go free ranging on your own. These quick writing forays are perfect for groups, and the last chapter takes you through the process of setting up and running a free-range writing group.

Note: All the poems mentioned in the poetry forays are freely available to read online, so you can simply google them.

Your free-range writing journal

By its very nature, everything you write on these free-range forays will be first thoughts and sketches. If, amongst it all, you stumble upon ideas, fragments or characters you want to investigate further, you can work on them and craft them up at a later time.

But keep your journal just for first thoughts and free-range writing. Cherish it, not because the pieces are good – they're experiments, with that lovely raw first draft energy – but because they're you, your life, your sensibility, your writer self.

Cross out, scribble in the margins, stick things in – don't worry in the slightest about writing beautifully, because all your writing is beautiful. First drafts like these are like rough diamonds, full of potential; polished final drafts have a different kind of beauty – love them all!

Get the most attractive notebook you can find, or buy a plain one and make it lovely. It feels like a rebellion to write freely and messily in a gorgeous notebook, and that's how to cherish and honour your wild writer's soul.

75 forays for the wild writer's soul

Memoir: The history of your writing

Did you like writing as a child? Was there someone who encouraged you – or someone who didn't? Have you ever kept a diary, or written a book? Have you ever wanted to?

What stories or poems do you remember writing? Did anyone read them?

How has your writing developed over the years, right up to the present moment?

Tell the story of your writing life. Take about fifteen minutes, just writing whatever comes. Don't try to plan or overthink it.

After fifteen minutes, go deeper. Notice what things you haven't chosen to mention. Write for another five minutes, exploring these.

This is your starting point. Maybe you've written poetry all your life, won some prizes, belonged to poetry groups. Or maybe you've kept a diary since you were a child, or written magazine articles, or spent the last decade working on a novel.

As well as recognising your normal writing tracks, notice also the directions you have never taken.

Let your free-range writing adventures begin!

Fiction: The stranger on the bridge

Before you read a single word about the task, I'm guessing the title will have conjured an image in your mind. What kind of bridge is it? Who else is on the bridge?

Pan back to take in the whole setting. What time of day is it? What time of year?

Is it an urban area or somewhere in the country?

What buildings, vehicles and other people can you see?

Take your time to fully picture the scene.

Now zoom in again, to the stranger on the bridge. See their face.

Move towards them.

Who are you, the person who comes upon the stranger? What are you doing on the bridge? Is it an arranged meeting, or complete happenstance?

Tell the story of this encounter, from coming on to the bridge, to leaving it.

Take twenty minutes.

Fiction tip

Whenever you're writing fiction, especially if it's a very short timed piece like this, don't worry about getting the beginning right. Just dive in!

Getting the beginning right is almost always a redrafting task because it's only when you've got the whole story that you know the best way for it to begin.

| 3 |

Non-Fiction: How to...

Make a list of things you know how to do, such as organising a social event, working on a checkout or looking after your garden.

Choose one.

Picture somebody in your mind that might like to learn this skill – it could be someone you know, or a made-up person of the kind who might be interested. For example, your niece who's just moved into their first house with a garden, a young family wanting to grow their own food or an older person struggling to maintain their garden.

Write a title that reflects your choice of reader: 'How to plan your first garden', 'How to grow enough vegetables to feed the whole family', 'How to make your garden easier to manage'.

Write the article, keeping your reader firmly in mind. Imagine you are talking to them. What questions might they ask you? What specifically would they like to know?

Take about twenty minutes.

Non-fiction tip

As with fiction, don't worry about getting the beginning right. You'll almost always want to tweak it after you've finished the piece because then you'll know exactly what you're introducing and what you want the voice of the piece to be.

Poetry: You are...

Think of someone you know – it can be anyone, a family member, friend, neighbour, teacher... It might be someone who's died, someone you haven't seen for a long while, or someone you see every day. It might be someone you love, someone you like, someone you don't know well or someone you dislike.

Go with the first person that pops into your head – however random!

Thinking about this person, if they were a kind of plant, what would they be? Write it down. Don't over-think it; go with your first idea, and be specific – there's a big difference between a wild rose in a hedgerow and a tea rose in a formal flowerbed.

Now jot down your first thoughts on these questions:

- What kind of animal would they be?

- What kind of tree?

- What kind of music?

- Season of the year?

- Kind of weather?

- Time of day?

- Item of clothing?

- Kind of landscape? (For example, forest, desert, urban).

- Kind of water? (For example, stream, ornamental pond, mountainous sea).

- Food?

- Drink?

Write a poem about the person, beginning 'You are...' and using some of the objects you have come up with for them. Don't try to make it rhyme unless it wants to, because focusing on regular patterns of rhyme and rhythm can draw your attention away from the images and emotion of the poem. You can repeat 'You are...' as often as you like. Take about twenty minutes.

Here's an example:

<u>My Friend Chris</u>

You are Sunday afternoon on a frosty hill
Fast water gurgling under the ground
Boots crunching through icy puddles
Heather sparkling, white breath hanging
You are laughter spilling into the air
Gloves rubbed together, quilted arms
You are a close hug under a wide, open sky

Fiction tip

You can use this method for creating characters
in a story or to get to know your characters better.

Choice: A day out

Where do you like to go on a day out? The shopping centre? The beach? A park? A visitor attraction? Write a list, and be specific – which shopping centre, beach, park or visitor attraction? Name them.

Choose one – the first one that takes your fancy. Don't over-think it.

Close your eyes, take a few slow breaths, and imagine you're there.

What time of day is it? What time of year? Use all your senses – notice what you can see and hear around you, the smell of the air, the feel of the ground beneath your feet. Take your time.

When you have fully imagined this familiar place, choose one of the following ways to use it in your writing. Take about twenty minutes.

Fiction

Somebody has come to this place to meet someone. Who is it, and how do they feel about the meeting?

The person they are meeting doesn't show up. How does your character feel? What do they decide to do? What happens next?

Memoir

Tell the story of one occasion when you went to this familiar place.

Non-fiction

Imagine you are writing an article for a tourist brochure. Your angle will depend upon who you're trying to attract – families, retired people, honeymoon couples...

Describe the place and give several reasons why your chosen kind of reader will love to visit it.

Poetry

The title of your poem will include the name of the place you're writing about. If you're going for a light or comic effect, you can give it a regular rhythm and rhyme. Otherwise use free verse to describe the place, and let the poem move into a specific time when you were there.

All genres tip

What is familiar to you will not be familiar to your readers, so use it. Take them to the places you know well. It's interesting for them and also a pleasure for you, because it helps you notice what is unique and interesting to others in your ordinary every day life.

Memoir: I remember...

Write whatever comes into your head beginning, 'I remember...' Keep your pen moving on the paper for fifteen minutes. When one strand of memory runs out, start again with the prompt, 'I remember...' and follow another one.

After fifteen minutes, reflect on what you've written. Notice what you've left out. Starting with 'I remember' again, focus on this for a further five minutes.

Finish on a light note – start 'I remember' again, and write for five minutes about things in your recent past that made you feel happy. They don't have to be huge events. Seeing a new bird at your bird feeder, getting an email from an old friend, trying a new recipe... There can be great pleasure in small things.

Memoir tip

Writing about difficult times in your earlier life can feel emotionally overwhelming. You want to remember those emotions, because they are the key to powerful writing, but it may be helpful to re-centre yourself when you have finished by reflecting upon the positive aspects of your current life.

You aren't the same person now as you were then; you are bigger, just as your life then is only part of the whole span of your life now.

Fiction: Feeling bad, feeling better

Someone is rocked by a difficult emotion. What is it? For example, jealousy, anger, boredom, fear.

Why are they feeling this way? What caused it?

Take a moment to imagine you are feeling this emotion. Notice the physical effects – where do you feel it in your body?

Stories are always about a protagonist who wants something. Your protagonist wants to stop feeling this way. What needs to happen in order for them to feel better? How can they make that happen?

Write the story of how they try to change their situation, ending in either success or failure. What do they learn? How does the journey change them?

Take about thirty minutes.

Fiction tip

When you are writing stories, as well as the action of the plot, think about the psychological journey of the protagonist. How are they changed by what has happened?

Non-Fiction: An interview with yourself

Write an interview with yourself. It will take the form of question and answer, for example:

Q   When did you know you wanted to be a funeral celebrant?

A   It was after my mother died...

Start with a few sentences of introduction about yourself, as if you are the interviewer. For example, 'Jenny Alexander is an author who...'

Ask the questions that will let you say what's most interesting about your life, and keep them short. Take longer over your answers. Enjoy being in the spotlight, even though you've put yourself there!

Fiction tip

You can use this interview technique to build your characters or get to know them better. Imagine you met them; what would you want to know? Write the Q and A.

Poetry: I am... I once... I will...

In your home or, if you have one, your garden, look around and pick any object, whichever calls to you – an ornament, maybe, a bowl, a pebble.

Hold it in your hands and examine it, using all your senses. Write for three minutes, describing your object.

Close your eyes and imagine you are the object. Feel your physical shape, size, weight.

Imagine you're in your normal environment – on the shelf, in the cupboard, on the path. What can you see and hear around you? Notice the smell of the air and the feel of the surface you're resting on.

How are you feeling emotionally? What colour is your mood?

Write for three minutes, whatever comes, as your object, beginning 'I am...'

Write for another three minutes, as your object, beginning 'I once...' Where have you come from? What have you seen?

Finally write for three minutes beginning 'I will...'

Reduce each of your three paragraphs down to one sentence, beginning 'I am', 'I once', 'I will.

Those are your warm-ups, just to get in the zone. You won't necessarily include them in your poem.

Now write a poem about your object. Use the three prompts – 'I am', 'I once', 'I will' – and write as the object, or change the prompts to 'You are/ once/will' and write in the second person. Alternatively, you could change the prompts to 'It is/once/will' and write in the third person, or not use the prompts at all, but start by describing the object and just see where it goes.

Play around with it; try it different ways, but stop after 15 minutes, choose your best version and give it a title. Have you captured the physicality and personality of your object? If not, do a few tweaks.

Choice: The lie

Lying leads to practical and moral complications and that makes it a brilliant theme for every kind of writing. Choose one of the following tasks, and write for about twenty minutes.

Memoir

Everyone has been lied to at some point in their life, sometimes over a long period of time. Think of an occasion when someone has lied to you. How did you find out they were lying? How did you feel about it? What did you do?

Now think of an occasion when you have told someone a lie. Why did you do it? Did they find out?

Decide which one you'd like to recount, and tell the story.

Fiction

Someone tells a lie – why? How do they feel about it? Who do they tell it to?

What are the consequences? Do they get found out?

Switching protagonists, think about this lie from the point of view of the person who has been lied to. Do they know they've been lied to? How do they know? When do they realise it? What are the consequences for them?

Decide whose point of view feels more interesting to you and write the story.

Non-fiction

Think of three occasions when it might be acceptable to tell a lie, such as telling someone you like their new hairstyle in order to protect their feelings, or telling a small child that Santa will come down the chimney and fill their stocking in order to create a magical experience of Christmas for them.

Jot down both the examples and the reasons why you might feel that, in these cases, lying might be acceptable.

Now think of three occasions when it would feel absolutely unacceptable to tell a lie, and include the reasons why. For example, claiming a neighbour's parcel that had been delivered to you had never arrived because you wanted to keep it, or telling a vegetarian there is no meat in the meal you have prepared because you don't believe in vegetarianism.

Compare your lists. What is it that makes a lie either acceptable or unacceptable?

Use some of your examples to build an opinion piece with the title, 'Is it ever right to tell a lie?'

Poetry

Write a poem that begins 'You said' or 'I said.' Repeat that starter as many times as you like throughout the poem.

End with the line, 'It wasn't true.' Use those words at other points in the poem too, if you like.

Memoir: But one particular day...

Write a list of all the houses you have lived in. Add any houses you used to spend a lot of time in – for example, one of mine might be my grandparents' house, where we spent every Saturday morning when my mother was working.

Choose one, and start with a description of the house, giving a general overview of the times you spent there. What was the pattern of your time there – what were your normal activities and preoccupations? Who else was around?

Move on from this general scene setting in place and time to tell the story of one particular thing that happened in that house that was out of the ordinary. For example, the evening you were having dinner with your family in the front room when a burglar came in by the back door, or the time your mother's best friend popped round for tea as usual, but broke the news that she had cancer, or the day your father came home with a puppy in his pocket.

Take about twenty minutes in total.

Fiction: Writing the intense moment

Write a five-point character sketch for your protagonist:

1. The character's name.

2. Their age and appearance.

3. Something they love.

4. Something they hate.

5. Something that's special to them.

Do this without thinking. Just go with the first ideas that come into your head. You might not use the information in your story, but these five points will help you get a sense of the person.

Ask your protagonist:

- 'What is the best thing that has happened to you?'

- 'What is the worst thing that has happened to you?'

- 'What is the funniest thing that has happened to you?'

Go with the first answers they come up with.

Write the story of one of these intense moments, the best, worst or funniest thing that has ever happened to your protagonist. For example, the first time she stepped onto the West End stage/ the moment he realised his wife was cheating on him/ the day she tipped a heaped plate of spaghetti into her mother-in-law's lap (by accident, of course!)

Take about twenty minutes.

Non-Fiction: Life's lessons

You don't have to be old to write as an elder, passing on things you've learnt from life rather than through academic learning.

What are the most important lessons you have learnt from life? For example, that everything passes, both the good times and the bad; that the most important thing in every kind of relationship is communication and that there is deep joy in giving.

Write for fifteen minutes, just whatever comes. Don't overthink it.

When the fifteen minutes is up, read back over what you've written and jot down the three main points. Write one sentence about each of them.

All genres tip

Reading back over what you've written and seeing the main points is good practice. It enables you to organise your ideas, build on what matters and cut out anything extraneous when redrafting.

Poetry: Ways to get rich

Write a list poem with ideas about how to get rich. Use either the second person – 'You could... Or you could' – or the first person, 'I could... Or I could...'

Round it off with a section beginning, 'But...' What if none of those ways worked? What if one of them did, and you got rich?

Take ten minutes to write your poem and a further ten minutes playing around with different drafts. Experiment with the way you organise the words into lines and arrange the lines on the page. Add some new ideas; take some away.

If it's funny, could you make it funnier? If it's serious, could you make it more thoughtful? Try different titles on for size; often, playing with title can give you new ideas, or even a whole new angle.

Poetry tip

One time when rhyme and a regular beat can be more effective than free verse is when your intention is humorous.

Choice: Three words

Make some lists of words under these headings: Colours, Emotions, Objects, Places, Jobs, Hobbies. Take about thirty seconds for each.

Ponder your lists for a few moments, and jot down any ideas for writing fiction, non-fiction, memoir or poetry that start to stir.

Decide which one you're going to develop into a story, article, poem or autobiographical piece.

Write it for about twenty minutes, trying to include one word from each of two of your lists in your first sentence. These might not go together in any obvious way, for example, irritation and apple pie.

Include a word from another list somewhere in the rest of the piece. Irritation... apple pie... camping.

All genres tip

Playing around with random ideas is a great way of breaking the assumption that you can only write when you feel inspired. You can write about anything, any time, and in any way you choose!

Memoir: Dear Diary

Think back to an earlier time in your life – when you were at primary school, perhaps, or in the early days of your career, or when your children had just flown the nest.

Recall where you lived at that time – the house, inside and outside, and the surrounding area.

What was a typical day for you? Who did you see? Where did you go? What did you eat? How did you spend your evenings?

Imagine you are back there. What time of year is it? What clothes are you wearing? What does it feel like to be in your body? Take your time.

Write a diary entry, as this younger self, recounting a normal day when nothing out of the ordinary has happened. Put the date, time and place at the top of your page and write for about twenty minutes.

Memoir and fiction tip

When you're writing in diary form, whether as a character in a story or your younger self in memoir, or indeed in your day-to-day diaries now, it can help to begin, 'Dear Diary...' and imagine you're writing a letter to a friend you haven't spoken to for a while.

You can always edit the 'Dear Diary' out at the redrafting stage, if you like. Anne Frank actually named her diary, and started her entries, 'Dear Kitty...'

Fiction: The put-down

Someone is trying to learn a new skill.

Who is it? Write some notes about your protagonist – name, age, appearance and anything else that strikes you as interesting.

What is the skill they are trying to learn? How are they going about it? Who else is involved?

In your story, your protagonist feels they are learning well, and have grasped the basics, but someone else criticises their achievement.

Who criticises it? What's their relationship to your protagonist? What do they say? What reaction are they hoping for?

How does your protagonist respond?

Write this scene for about twenty minutes.

Non-Fiction: Valentine's Day Q and A

If Valentine's Day doesn't do it for you, choose a different one, such as Mother's Day, Boxing Day, Remembrance Sunday or May Day.

Start by writing a list of questions about it that you don't already know the answers to, such as 'Who was St Valentine?', 'When did people start celebrating his day?', 'Is Valentine's Day recognised throughout the world?', 'Why are Valentine's cards traditionally anonymous… or actually, are they traditionally anonymous?!'

Research and find out the answers.

Write a Q and A piece, including the five most interesting things you discover.

Non-fiction tip

One of the joys of writing non-fiction is noticing and filling in the gaps in your own knowledge, gaps you may not even have been aware of before.

Poetry: Similes, fresh and funny

Similes are part of the symbolic language of poetry, expanding the meaning of one thing by likening it to another.

We use them in everyday speech – 'as big as a bus,' 'as bald as a coot', 'as clean as a whistle' – but these clichés are so devalued we hardly even notice them, let alone feel struck by their meaning.

Some feel old-fashioned, like 'as bright as a button' – that would have worked better when buttons were made of brass and polished – or 'as bent as a nine-bob note', which would leave anyone outside the UK or under forty scratching their head.

Some are meaningless to almost everyone – what even is a sand-boy, and why is he happy? (In case you're wondering, a sand-boy was a male worker of low status, a 'boy', whose job was to deliver sand to hostelries for spreading on bar room floors before sawdust became the thing, and sand-boys were happy because innkeepers often gave them ale).

Start by completing some common clichés to get in the zone:

1. As happy as... (there are others besides sandboys!)

2. As big as...

3. As sound as...

4. As steady as...

5. As strong as...

6. As rich as...

7. As wise as...

8. As cool as...

9. As fresh as...

10. As easy as...

Don't worry if you've got gaps, and if you can think of several for the same one, write them all.

Now get creative, forget about clichés and invent several fresh similes of your own. For a bonus point, try to get some that alliterate – as skinny as a ski pole, as frisky as a fly on a fairy cake, as silly as a singing sandwich.

Finally, make up some funny ones, by putting opposites together, instead of comparing like to like – as happy as a fish in a sandpit, as cool as a sausage in a sauna, as wild as Wiltshire on a Wednesday night.

Poetry, fiction and memoir tip

Playing around with similes is a great mental workout and they aren't only the stuff of poetry; you can use them to enrich your prose pieces too.

Choice: A conversation

Choose one of the following tasks, and take about twenty minutes for the writing.

Memoir

Think of a time when you were engaged in an activity with someone else and they said something that upset you, or you said something that upset them.

Run through the conversation in your mind, as fully as you can, including what you were both doing at the time.

Write the scene using as much dialogue as possible. Embed the dialogue in the action so the reader knows exactly what you're both doing as the conversation unfolds.

If you prefer, recount a conversation you've witnessed or overheard, where one person said something that upset or offended the other, telling not only what was said, but also how the activity they were engaged in unfolded.

Fiction

Two people are working on something together. For example, decorating a room, preparing a meal, putting together a plan or proposal.

Who are they, and what are they doing? Write some notes.

One says something that upsets the other. What do they say, and how does the other respond?

Write the scene using as much dialogue as possible. Embed the dialogue in the action:

> 'What do you mean?' Ellen said, putting down her pen.
> Martha went on ticking things off her lists. 'Oh, I think you know.'

Non-fiction

Do a question and answer piece, where you make up the questions and then answer them, on a topic of your choice. For example:

Q   Why is hairdressing always top of the league for happiness at work?

A   It's a combination of things. Hairdressing requires on-going training and professional development, and job satisfaction is highest in careers where people get to use their   skills. It's also a very sociable job.

Q   What are the main health concerns for hairdressers?

A   They're on their feet all day, so...

Poetry

Write a poem about a conversation. It may be one you've made up, overheard or actually taken part in. Before you start, as with all passages of dialogue, fully imagine the action of the scene, not just the words that are spoken.

Fiction and memoir tip

When you're writing dialogue, think of it as writing a scene, not just an exchange of words. Dialogue isn't an adornment; it's part of the action, and should always move the action along.

If you hold this focus you'll avoid slowing your plot down with pointless exchanges about the weather or how many sugars your protagonist likes in his tea. That might be the stuff of real-life conversations, but you're telling a story, not transcribing real life.

Memoir: Didn't we have a lovely time?

Didn't we have a lovely time, the day we went to... Where? And who went? Think of a few great days out you've had, any time in the past.

Then consider the sentence substituting 'lovely' with horrible/boring/exciting, and think of some examples for each of those.

Choose one and tell the story. Exaggerate the mood of the day; if it was boring, make it sound like the most boring day ever, if exciting, the most exciting, and so on.

Take about twenty minutes.

Fiction: Out in the cold

Someone is shutting someone out.

Who, and who are they shutting out? Write some character notes.

Why are they shutting them out?

What makes them stop, and let the person in?

What happens when they do?

Write the story. Twenty minutes.

Non-Fiction: Top tips

Begin with some lists:

- Places you've been on holiday

- Kinds of holiday you've had, for example, camping, hotel, holiday village, Airbnb

Imagine someone who's never been to that place or had that kind of holiday is asking you for your advice. What kind of person are they – their social and financial situation, age and temperament?

List all the tips you might give this person, and choose the best five.

Give your piece a title, for example, 'Five top tips for your first camping trip', 'Five top tips for a successful city break', 'Five top tips for your day trip to London.'

Write a sentence of introduction, such as, 'Camping can be great fun for families, but if you're planning your first camping trip, here are some things to bear in mind...'

Write a sentence in conclusion to round it up. 'If you choose a family-friendly site where there are indoor activities nearby for rainy days, take spare blankets to put under your sleeping bags... etc, you'll have a wonderful time!'

Poetry: Don't tell me...

This poem will begin with the words, 'Please, don't tell me.'

Who tells you things you don't want to hear? For example, I know someone who likes to tell me about her many and various ailments, what the doctor said and didn't say, what the tablets do and don't do – you probably know someone like that too!

Or maybe you know someone who gives you unwanted advice, or rams their political opinions down your throat, or tells you intimate details of their personal life and makes you feel uncomfortable.

Go with the first person that comes into your head. What do they tell you, and why don't you want to hear it?

What would you rather they talked to you about?

Choose free verse or rhyming, as the mood takes you. Twenty minutes.

Choice: Fire

Fire is paradoxically a source of comfort and of danger, and both of those provoke very strong emotions. So, all in all, it's a great inspiration for writing.

Choose one of these tasks. Take about twenty minutes.

Memoir

What happy memories do you have about sitting around a fire? For me, one would be camping on a beach in Shetland and building a driftwood fire in a circle of stones when I was newly married. Another would be Saturday evenings when my children were small, having tea and toast round the fire after a family day out.

What exciting memories do you have of fire? For me, the day the compost heap burst into flames and the fire engine came – I was three or four years old.

What alarming memories? My dressing gown caught fire when I was little, and my mother tore the curtain down and wrapped me up in it. Another time, when I was in my teens, we were all woken up in the night by what sounded like bombs going off. It was a fire at a bottled gas yard, several miles away, and the gas cylinders were all exploding.

Choose one, and tell the story.

Fiction

Something is on fire – for example, a kitchen, a house, a school, a shop, a rubbish dump, an area of heathland.

How did the fire start? Did someone cause it, either by accident or on purpose? Is anyone in danger? Is anyone hurt?

Somebody takes action. Do they get help? Do they try to tackle the flames on their own? Do they try to rescue someone, or retrieve a precious object?

Write the story.

Non-fiction

Write an article about fire safety. Focus on one kind of fire, such as the do's and don'ts of building a bonfire or having a barbecue. Include what to do in the event of an accident.

Poetry

The hearth is the heart of the home – or at least, it used to be, before we had central heating.

Picture a parlour in times gone by. The heavy curtains are drawn against the chilly night. This is before television, so the focal point of the room is the fireplace, where a coal fire is burning brightly.

Look around. Examine the furniture, the floor coverings, and the pictures on the wall. Notice the sound of the fire, and the dancing light of the flickering flames across the ceiling and walls.

Write a poem. Give it an old style feel, with a regular rhythm and rhyme. If you like, check out Clement Clarke Moore's poem, *Twas The Night before Christmas,* before you start, to get you in the mood.

Memoir: The history of shoes in your life

Write a list of shoes you recall wearing at different stages in your past. You're likely to remember a lot from your childhood and young adult years, but try to include some from more recent times as well. Have a good ponder. Take about five minutes.

Choose half a dozen, either from one particular period or from different stages in your life. Memoirs can span a lifetime or a couple of years, or even less.

Write the history of these shoes, considering each pair one at a time. Describe them in detail. How old were you when you wore them? Where did you walk in them? How did wearing them make you feel?

Take about five minutes for each one.

Note: You might also like to try this great suggestion from beta reader, Liz – 'Could this perhaps include shoes of people in your life too? My mother had a pair of patent leather evening shoes I used to call her petrol shoes as they had the same rainbow sheen as spilt petrol. Or the heavily used shoes of a parent, family member… broken shoes…'

When I read this, I immediately thought of the flip flops my friend was wearing in a tea garden in Clovelly the last time I saw her before she was diagnosed with a terminal illness.

I like this variation because writing about someone else's shoes will not only say a lot about them but also about you, and about the relationship between you.

Fiction: I am writing to complain...

Someone has a bee in their bonnet! Who?

What has annoyed them?

Imagine you are this person. What thoughts are going round and round in your head? What words does your inner voice use to describe them? Notice where you feel your annoyance in your body.

Write some notes.

As your character, write a letter of complaint. Who are you writing to? What do you want them to do?

Think about the voice of your letter as you write; use the kind of language your character would use.

If you're going for comic effect, exaggerate their outrage and make their demands disproportionate. Anger and indignation are a gift for comedy writing – think Victor Meldrew and Hyacinth Bucket!

Take about five minutes for the notes and fifteen for the letter.

Non-Fiction: A review

Reviewing used to be the province of professionals, but now we can all be reviewers on sites such as Amazon and TripAdvisor. Writing a review is a good way of organising your thoughts and understanding your own responses to the world.

Start with some lists:

- Films and TV shows you love.

- Films and TV shows you hate.

- Books you have read and remembered, either because you really enjoyed them or because you really didn't.

- Places you have visited.

- Hotels and restaurants you have stayed and/or eaten in.

Choose one thing from one of your lists to write about.

Decide on your angle – are you going to own it as your opinions and feelings by using the first person, 'I' and 'me', or present it as objective? Give your review a title. For example, 'This book changed my life', 'A book that can change people's lives.'

Write the review for ten minutes, backing up what you say with examples – 'The menu is basic and over-priced – we ended up paying £6.99 for macaroni cheese, and it wasn't even very tasty...'

When you've finished, identify the most important points and reduce it down to a couple of sentences.

All genres tip

Reviewing goods and services is an opportunity to publish your writing and, as with anything you write, it's a good idea to set your work aside for a while before you put it out there.

'Resting' a finished piece has two advantages: firstly, you often find fresh and pithy ideas come to you, seemingly out of the blue, once you've done all the thinking and writing it takes to complete a draft and secondly, you can see more clearly how to make it better once you've got a little distance on it.

Poetry: A madeleine

In his monumental memoir, *Remembrance of Things Past*, Marcel Proust describes the moment a whole period of his life came vividly back to him when he bit into a madeleine, dipped in tea.

This little cake had been a regular feature of his childhood teatimes though he had forgotten that detail, along with most of the details of his early life, until he happened to eat one, decades later. The idea that we can unlock lost memories through the senses is nowadays well established.

Choose a food you have in the house – it could be something you love, something you're not that keen on, or even something you find unpleasant.

Examine it closely, noticing its colours and textures. Pick it up and feel the weight of it, and the way its surfaces feel in your fingers. Notice any physical effects you feel, just looking at it. Does it make your mouth water, for example?

Close your eyes and eat a bit. Savour it. Notice how it feels on your lips, and in your mouth and throat. What thoughts and memories come into your mind as you're eating?

Write a poem. Take twenty minutes.

Poetry and memoir tip

Simply remembering what you used to eat at different times in your life will bring back other memories, because food is such a central part of everyone's experience. If you can source and taste something you haven't eaten for years, you may find it triggers memories even more powerfully.

Choice: Looking for love

A growing percentage of people use online dating sites and apps to look for love, and that is the theme of this task. Choose one of the following. Once you've made some notes, write for about twenty minutes.

Memoir

If you have tried online dating, tell the story of one of your dates. If you haven't tried it personally but you know someone who has, write the story of them telling you about their experiences, and what you thought and felt about it.

Fiction

Picture a person using an online site or app. What are they looking for – a companion, a bit on the side, a long-term relationship?

Read through their profile. What do they say about themselves? Are they honest?

Look closely at the photo they've chosen to include. Why did they choose that particular one? What do they think it says about them? What will it actually say to other people using the site?

Someone else likes their profile – who?

Write the story of their first meeting, and the build-up to it.

Non-fiction

Either research some facts and figures about online dating and write an article based on a numbered list, or draw on your own experience to write a piece on how to go about it, some top tips or dos and don'ts. Give examples to back up your ideas.

Poetry

Write a narrative poem telling the story of your own adventure/s in online dating, or as a fictional character telling theirs. Use rhyme and rhythm if it's a funny story; otherwise keep it free, as this helps the thoughts, images and feelings to develop and flow.

Memoir: Mother

Write about your mother for twenty minutes, whatever comes. It doesn't have to hold together so, if one line of thought runs out, just start with another, and keep your pen moving on the paper until the time is up.

Twenty minutes is not long to talk about one of the most significant people in your life, so let your mind follow whatever trails it wants to. It may surprise you.

Fiction: Better than they thought

This is a scene in which somebody surprises him/herself by acting in a way they didn't realise they had in them.

Begin by writing a list of human weaknesses. For example, a tendency to interfere, unkindness, cowardice.

Create a character that strongly identifies with one of these characteristics. You need to know their name, age and appearance.

Put them in a situation where that quality would normally be activated. For example, give an interfering busybody an opportunity to interfere, or put a cowardly one in a situation where they would normally run away.

Have them react in an uncharacteristic way, and surprise themselves.

What are the consequences? How do they feel about it? What do they do about it? What do they learn?

Write the scene for about twenty minutes.

Fiction tip

Everyone is capable of surprising themselves and the people who know them. Once you have established the character of your protagonist, remember that you can have them behave in a surprising way too.

Non-Fiction: I love...

Your interests and passions can energise your writing, whatever genre you're working in. For this piece of non-fiction, start by writing whatever comes into your head for five minutes, from the prompt, 'I love...'

Include anything except specific people, for example, places, pastimes and activities. Repeat the prompt as often as you like.

Choose one of the things you've mentioned, and write an article about it. Start with a sentence of introduction, saying what your article is about and expressing your enthusiasm – 'I love St Ives so much, I go there every year...', 'Salsa dancing is a wonderful way to de-stress when life feels fraught...', 'My kids love scuba diving – so will yours!'

Explain what you love about your subject, giving examples from your own life. Round it off with a concluding sentence that sums your article up. 'So if you're holidaying in Cornwall, you'll definitely want to visit St Ives!'

Take about fifteen minutes.

Poetry: Waking up

Write a list of places you know well, such as your local library or theatre, your grandparents' house, Brighton Beach, Manchester Airport, the cottage in Wales you stayed in last year – whatever random places come to mind.

Choose one for the setting of your poem.

What are the dominant colours in that setting?

What are the dominant shapes and forms?

What clothing would you wear there?

Make some notes.

Now imagine you are in that setting; you have been asleep – maybe all night, or for a couple of hours, or maybe you just nodded off for a few minutes. As you wake into that place, what are the first things that come into your awareness?

How do you feel emotionally, waking in that place? Where do you feel those emotions in your body?

What can you see and hear? Notice the smell of the air and the feel of the surface you' are sitting or lying on. Use all your senses.

Write a poem. Come to it with a relaxed mind, allowing it to evolve, like emerging into wakefulness. Let it flow, avoiding any regular patterns of rhythm and rhyme.

Don't try to make it good. Just enjoy!

Take about twenty minutes.

Choice: An interview

Everyone has had the experience of being interviewed, and some people of interviewing others. Different jobs call for different kinds of interview, from the informal chat with one other person to the formal panel; some are over in minutes, while others may be spread over several days.

Besides applying for jobs, there are many other interview situations. Prospective students may be selected by interview; researchers may gather evidence through interviews; oral exams are interviews of a kind, and interviews may be part of the vetting process for some membership organisations.

Choose one of these tasks on the subject of interviews. Write for about twenty minutes.

Memoir

Think of some interview situations you've been in, either as interviewer or interviewee. Choose one and take a few moments to fully recall it.

What was the room like? The furniture? The flooring?

Who was present? What were they wearing?

Was there anything you noticed in particular?

Remember how you felt, both physically and emotionally, before, during and after the interview. What questions were asked? What answers were given? What was the outcome?

Write the story.

Fiction

Someone is going for an interview and, when they walk into the room, they realise they know the interviewer or someone on the interviewing panel.

Who is going for the interview? Who do they recognise? Write some character notes. Where have they met before, and what is the relationship between them?

How do they handle the situation? Do they disclose that they know each other, or keep quiet about it? What are the reasons for their decision? Are they both of the same mind, or does one want to say something but the other one doesn't? What is the outcome?

Decide whose point of view feels most interesting to you, and write the story in the first person, either as the interviewer or the interviewee.

Non-fiction

Think of an interview situation. Imagine you are the interviewer, or work for the interviewing organisation. Write an advice sheet for prospective interviewees to enclose with their letter of invitation. Use the title, 'How to prepare for your interview.'

To get the content and tone right, you will need to be clear about who you are writing for. What kind of person would be going for this particular job, participating in this piece of research or whatever? Think about their age and level of education.

Start by describing the interview process and what they can expect. Then offer advice on how they can best prepare, and how they will be informed about the result.

Poetry

Here are five of the most common interview questions:

- What can you tell me about yourself?

- Why do you want to work here?

- Can you list your strengths?

- What are your weaknesses?

- Where do you see yourself five years from now?

Choose one to use as your first line, and write a poem about an interview, either from the point of view of the interviewer or of the interviewee.

You could focus your whole poem on just that one question, and repeat it if you want to. If you prefer, you could structure your poem around several or all of the questions.

Memoir: Your future self

The charm of memoir is not so much in the events that happen as in the particular psyche of the author, how they understand and respond to what happens to them.

The future, like the past, is part of the self in the present. Just as we are built on past experiences, we are also built on future dreams.

Think of something you want to achieve, however unlikely it might seem. A dream doesn't have to be realistic to inform your life.

Fly forward in imagination; see yourself striving towards this goal and achieving success. How and when will you know you have succeeded?

This deserves a celebration!

How will you celebrate? It could be a party with all your friends, family or colleagues; it could be a private celebration, just you alone or with a few close people.

Close your eyes and imagine the scene. Use all your senses. How does it feel to have achieved this dream?

Where do you feel the emotion in your body? Savour the moment. Really enjoy it. Then write the scene for twenty minutes.

Fiction: Feel the feelings

We tend to think of emotions as somehow outside our physical experience, but they are always felt in the body.

If you describe the physical sensations of emotions rather than just stating how your characters feel, the reader feels these sensations in their body too, and this makes for much more effective writing.

For example, rather than saying, 'She felt scared', you could describe the physical effects of that emotion in her body. 'She caught her breath... the hairs on the back of her neck stood on end ...'

Instead of saying, 'He looked amazed', you might describe how that emotion affects the way his body looks. 'His jaw dropped... his eyes opened wide...'

Write for ten minutes from each of these story starters, describing the physical effects of the strong emotions the protagonists feel:

- 'Police!' I shouted into the phone. 'It's an emergency!'

- Jessica set the table for one...

- Rob reached out and took her hand...

When you have finished, check back and cross out any places where you have stated how they feel – 'He was horrified... She felt lonely... She was overcome by desire...' and so on. If you have shown how they feel in their physical symptoms, telling it should be unnecessary.

Non-Fiction: Facts

One of the pleasures of writing non-fiction is that it makes you expand your knowledge of things you're interested in. This task is about checking your facts and finding out new ones, a skill you will often need in writing fiction too, for developing themes and settings.

What subjects do you know a bit about? Think in terms of skills and interests, jobs and life experiences. Jot some down.

Choose one, and make a list of things you know about it.

Then write a list of things you don't know, as questions. Where did kickboxing originate? Is it an Olympic sport? What are the health risks and benefits?

Underline three of the things you know from your first list, and three of the things you don't know from the second.

Check the facts you know and look up the answers to the ones you don't. Double check information you find online by looking at several sources.

Feels good, doesn't it?

Poetry: The poetry persona

People commonly assume that poems represent the views and feelings of the poet, but this isn't necessarily so.

Make a list of things you feel strongly about. Go with the first half dozen or so that come into your head – for example, foxhunting, immigration, non-biodegradable packaging, local parking regulations, people clearing up after their dogs.

Choose one.

Imagine someone who holds the opposite view to your own – what kind of person would that be? Picture them. What age are they? What gender?

Hear them giving you a piece of their mind. How do they speak?

Now be that person. Imagine how it feels to be in that body, wearing those clothes, having that presence in the world.

As that person, write a poem about an incident or experience that supports your point of view on this issue. Do it in the first person, 'I', but remember the voice of this poem is their voice; it should not sound like you.

Write it quickly, off the top of your head. Then redraft it, focusing on making the emotions and personality of your narrator shine through in their words.

Choice: A meal

Mealtimes are a rich seam for writing in every genre, and there's a vast menu of possibilities to choose from: state banquets, family gatherings, romantic dinners, takeaways, birthday celebrations, TV dinners, snatched sandwiches at the computer…

Mealtimes may be sociable or solitary affairs. A whole group culture or an individual psyche can be expressed in people's relationships with food.

Choose one of the following tasks. Take about twenty minutes for the actual writing, after you've done the preparation.

Memoir

Think about your family mealtimes when you were a child, and how they evolved at different stages in your childhood. Where did you usually eat breakfast? Who was with you?

What about lunch – did you have school dinners? And teatime?

Were your mealtime customs the same at the weekends as during the week?

What was the atmosphere of your family mealtimes? How did you feel about them? What kind of thing did you eat, and how did you feel about your food?

Choose a period of your life, and the mealtime you'd like to write about, breakfast, lunch, tea or supper. Start by describing a typical occasion, setting it in the background of your family life at that time.

If you can remember one occasion in particular, move on to that, marking the change of focus with something like, 'But one day...'

Note: Nigel Slater uses this technique to great effect in his wonderful memoir, *Toast*.

Fiction

Someone is offered a food item they don't want to eat. Who? What is the item?

Why don't they want to eat it?

Who is offering it to them?

Where are they?

Who else is present?

Write some notes.

What does your protagonist do – accept it but leave it on the plate? Decline? Try it and spit it out? How do the people around them respond?

Think about how this little exchange over food, offered and rejected, might reflect the relationship between the characters concerned. Write the scene.

Non-fiction

Decide what kind of mealtime you would like to write about, for example, an intimate supper, a dinner party, or a Mothers' Day tea.

Write a how-to piece about the mealtime you have chosen, setting it out in the form of a recipe. Use 'How To' or 'A Recipe For' in the title, give a sentence of introduction, then organise it in sections under subheadings, 'You Will Need' and 'Method.' Sum it up with a sentence of conclusion.

You don't have to stick with the choosing and preparation of food, just because it's laid out as a recipe. Your article might be focused on other aspects of the occasion, such as 'How to Survive Sunday Lunch with the In-laws', 'A Family Picnic; Minimise the Hassle, Maximise the Fun!' or 'Supper à Deux: A Recipe for Romance.'

Poetry

Write a poem about a mealtime, starting 'She/he gave me...' or 'She/he gave he gave him/her...' or 'She/he gives them...' or 'She/he gives you...'

Make the bulk of your poem a list of foods, with as much or as little description as you like, giving the reader a sense of the people involved, their relationship and situation by the kind of food they're sharing and the language you use to describe it.

Memoir: Father

Write about your father for twenty minutes, just whatever comes. It doesn't have to hold together so, if one line of thought runs out, just start with another, and keep your pen moving on the paper until the time is up.

Twenty minutes is not long to talk about one of the most significant people in your life. You can't say everything, so just let your mind follow whatever trails it wants to, and see where it goes.

Fiction: Running

Someone is running away. Who?

What, or who, are they running away from?

What will happen if they get caught?

In this story they do get away. How? Will their escape be permanent, or just for now?

Write the story. Twenty minutes.

Non-Fiction: Selling

What objects do you really love having in your life? Your flat, your cat, your favourite coat, your bike, your antique writing desk…

Write down the first five things you think of.

Choose three of those five, and jot down what you love about them.

Choose one of those three and write about it for five minutes, just whatever comes, describing all its fine qualities.

That's the preparation.

Now imagine you have to sell the object. Write a sales pitch for it. Why would someone else want to have this particular object in their life? Take five minutes.

For the second part of this task, write a list of five objects in your life you would be happy to get rid of or exchange. Maybe you're fed up with your house, your car, those boots you've worn to death, the silver biscuit barrel that always needs polishing, your collection of unusual paperclips (what were you thinking?!)…

Choose three of those five, and jot down everything you don't like about them.

Choose one of those three and write about it for five minutes, just whatever comes, describing all its negative qualities.

That's the preparation. Now imagine you want to sell the object. Why would anyone want to have this particular object in their life? Take five minutes to write a sales pitch for it. This time, you'll have to be more creative!

Poetry: The best thing

Choose a really important relationship in your life to write about. Who is/was it with? What was the best thing you ever did for them? Go with your first thoughts.

Write a poem beginning, 'The best thing I ever did for (whoever)...' Don't plan it; just let it take you where it needs to go.

When you've found the general sense of your poem, play with the words until it finds a shape, form and sound that please you.

Note: You might like to start by reading Ron Padgett's poem, *The Best Thing I Did*. It begins 'The best thing I did for my mother...' and goes on to ponder the past, present and future of his relationship with her.

All genres tip

When you're writing poetry, you'll obviously want to test all the changes you make by reading aloud, because a poem is so much about the sound of the words, and also a poem is short enough to make that practicable.

But whatever you write, try to read it aloud all the way through at least once, because when you read out loud you can't skim over any places where the writing could flow better.

Choice: Physical illness

Everyone has some experience of physical illness, injury or disability, as a sufferer, a witness or a caregiver. Choose one of the following writing tasks on this universal topic.

Memoir

Make three lists:

- Physical illnesses, injuries or disabilities you have suffered at various times in your life.

- Physical illnesses, injuries or disabilities close friends or family members have suffered.

- Occasions when you have cared for someone suffering from physical illness, injury or disability.

Don't overthink it. You're not looking for the most significant examples, just the first ones that come into your head.

Choose one, and write about it for twenty minutes.

Fiction

Because the mind, body and spirit are all part of the same being, physical afflictions can reflect emotional states of being. Someone who is under a lot of stress may be accident prone, for example, or suffer from frequent headaches; an anxious person may develop digestive disorders, and an angry one high blood pressure.

This task is about creating a character who is suffering from a physical illness, injury or disability, where the nature of their ailment feels in line with their personality or situation.

What is the ailment? Jot down a few possibilities and choose one.

Who is suffering from it? Write some notes on their name, age and appearance.

What is their situation in life, and how does their particular affliction reflect this?

How do they feel about their ailment, and how do they cope with it? Who do they turn to for help?

Work on building up a clear picture of this character for about ten minutes. Then spend a further ten minutes jotting down ideas for other characters with physical illnesses, injuries or disabilities, to get a feel for how this can be a useful aspect of characterisation.

Non-fiction

Write an article about a physical illness, injury or disability that you know about, either as a sufferer, a witness or a caregiver.

This could take the form of objective advice on how to handle it, or a personal account of your own experience with the goal of helping other people who might be going through the same thing.

Take twenty minutes.

Poetry

Choose a physical illness, injury or disability you have personally suffered from.

Without over thinking, jot down the first one or two *physical objects* that come to mind for each of the following:

- What does it feel like? For example, deep mud, a needle or an overripe pear.

- What does it sound like? For example, a chainsaw, a mosquito or an old fridge.

- What does it smell like? For example, an empty house, a kitchen bin or a busy road.

- What does it look like? For example, a broken cup, a dead dog or a park bench.

- What does it taste like? For example, a lump of coal, a lemon, cold tea.

Choose one of these objects for your title – 'Dead Dog', 'The Kitchen Bin', 'A Mosquito.'

Set aside any thoughts of the illness, injury or disability, and focus on the object.

Write a poem about the object. Start by describing it, using all your senses, then put it in a setting and allow thoughts and ideas to develop from that.

Take about twenty minutes.

Note: You won't have referred to the illness or injury at all, but after you have finished, reflect back on whether your poem has given you any new insights into it.

Memoir: All your teachers

Teachers can have a great influence on a child or young person's life, for good or ill. Starting as far back as you can, write the names of all the teachers you can remember through school, college and any job training.

Underline three, and write for five minutes about each of them, whatever comes. Try to include at least one teacher you liked and one you didn't.

Choose one of your three teachers and write a letter to them. Tell them what you recall of their lessons, and the effect they've had on your life subsequently. Take about ten minutes.

Fiction: Something happened on the way to...

This story will use a journey that's familiar to you for the setting – a trail you've travelled at least once before, and maybe many times. Take a moment to think of one you'd like to use.

Imagine someone who is on that path/train/motorway/ whatever, and see them as if you're watching a film. Notice the scenery they're passing through, the time of day/year, the weather, the colours.

Stop the film, and study the still. Focus in on the person, and answer these questions:

- Who is it – man/woman/boy/girl?

- How old are they and what are they wearing?

- Have they made this journey before?

- Why are they making this journey now?

- What are they hoping to find at the end of it?

- Why does it matter that the journey ends the way they hope it will?

- One word to describe their mood

- What's made them feel that way?

Now you have a character, in a setting, something they hope for, and why it matters (stakes). That's the set-up.

So, to the action. Something happens that threatens to stop the character from completing the journey – a meeting, chance or planned, an accident, a thought or fear (the block can be inner, outer or both).

How does your character deal with it? Do they overcome the block and reach their destination? Do they get deflected and go somewhere else? Do they get there via a different route?

Does your character get what they hoped for and, if not, how do they cope with that result?

Write the scene for twenty minutes. At some point during the narrative, name the places your protagonist is travelling from and to, and give your story a title.

All genres tip

If you are thinking about real places when you write a poem or story, it can be a good idea to name them. Readers who have been there will enjoy recognising the references, and those who haven't may be interested to go.

The exception might be if you're setting fiction in a small village, because readers might think aspects of your story or the characters in it are based on real life too. (I met one writer who kicked a hornets' nest when she used her own real village as the setting for a rambunctious tale of wife swapping).

Non-Fiction: The problem with...

Take twenty minutes to sound off about all the things you feel disgruntled about.

Start 'The problem with...' and when one train of thought runs out, begin with a new one from the same prompt. 'The problem with...'

This should be an easy bit of non-fiction for anyone over about forty, but if you're young and full of the joys, you might have to get creative!

Poetry: Just this

Picture this: an empty room, except for one piece of furniture.

What is it? Describe it in detail for three minutes.

Why is the room empty? Why is this piece of furniture still in there? Who does it belong to? Make some notes.

Write a poem, either from the point of view of the piece of furniture, or as the room, or as the owner, or as another person who comes upon the scene.

Think about the mood and personality of the point-of-view character, because this will help you to find the voice.

Take about twenty minutes.

Choice: Gifts

Giving and receiving presents is a celebration of relationships as well as of occasions, and it can be accompanied by strong emotions of stress, anticipation, joy, pleasure, gratitude or disappointment.

Choose one of these writing tasks on the subject of gifts. Take about twenty minutes.

Memoir

Think of one example for each of the following, the first one that springs to mind, and jot it down.

An occasion when you received a gift that

- Disappointed you.

- Surprised you.

- Delighted you.

An occasion when you gave a gift that

- You felt you got right.

- You felt you got wrong.

- You felt unsure about giving.

If other occasions occur to you that don't fit these questions, jot them down. For example, did you ever expect to receive a gift but not receive it? Or not expect to receive one and wish it hadn't been given? Did you ever intend to give a gift, but fail to give it?

Choose one. Recall it to mind in as much detail as you can. Write the story.

Fiction

Someone has received a gift that wasn't what they wanted. Who, what and why? Write some notes.

Who gave it to them? How did they feel about giving it? What response did they expect? What response did they get? Write some notes.

What are the consequences for their relationship?

Tell the story from the point of view of either the giver or the receiver.

Non-fiction

I once blogged about ten great Christmas presents for writers. What groups might you have present ideas for?

Think about your social situation, hobbies and work. Jot down some ideas.

Choose one and write an article based on a numbered list, for example, ' Five awesome anniversary treats for your girlfriend', 'Seven great birthday presents for quilters', 'Ten Christmas gift Ideas for families on a budget.'

Start with a short introduction and include a sentence or two about each item on your list, saying why it would make the perfect gift.

Poetry

Think about all the different kinds of gifts there are; objects bought or made, words of love and encouragement, talents and personal qualities, grace and good fortune.

Every gift can carry both positive and negative possibilities. For example, loving words may be well meaning but badly received; good fortune may mean you have farther to fall.

Write a poem about a gift, exploring both its brightness and its shadow side. You could focus on the physical object and allow ideas to develop from that, or make it a more abstract, philosophical piece and allow concrete images to develop from the ideas.

Keep it fluid, with no fixed rhyme or rhythm, and see where it takes you.

Memoir: The view from your window

Think back to your childhood bedroom, the earliest one you can remember. Close your eyes and take yourself back there. Be in your child body, in your child clothes.

Glance back at the room behind you as you walk across to the window and look out.

What can you see? What time of year is it? What's the weather like? Sit quietly and take it in.

Think of a specific occasion when you were looking out of that window and something happened. It might be something small and everyday, such as one of your parents leaving for work, or your sister playing in the garden with the girl next door.

Write a description of the scene.

Now think of the next bedroom you can remember, and repeat the exercise. Keep going through all your bedrooms, right up to the present day, or until the time runs out.

Take thirty minutes.

Fiction: A life in five days

Someone has reached a turning point in their life. For example, they might be about to turn fifty, or have their first baby, get married or divorced, begin a new job, move house or lose a close friend.

Who? And what is the turning point? Write some character notes – their name, age, appearance, where they live, who they live with and anything else that comes to mind.

As your character reflects back from this pivotal moment and considers how they got here, what are the main events they remember?

This story consists of five brief scenes, snapshot moments of something that happened, like stills in the movie of their life up to this point.

For example, for someone going through a divorce, these might include a scene from his childhood that shows his parents' relationship, then the first time he met his soon-to-be-ex wife, his wedding day, a row about their growing children and finally the start of his affair.

Take about five minutes to ponder and make some notes, and five minutes to write each scene.

Non-Fiction: The best of times, the worst of times

Why is this year the very best time to be alive? Write persuasively for ten minutes, just as it comes, explaining all the reasons you can think of.

Change tack and write for another ten minutes, explaining why this is the worst year ever.

With both pieces, exaggerate. Don't be afraid of being dishonest or misleading. This is the post truth era, after all.

Non-fiction tip

Whenever you are writing a factual piece, exploring the opposite point of view at the planning stage can help you develop your argument by showing you where the case needs to be made.

It might also, on occasions, lead to you modifying or changing your position if you find the opposite case to be actually quite convincing.

Poetry: The proposal

Somebody makes a proposal. Who?

What are they proposing?

Who are they proposing it to?

Take a few moments to picture the scene. Hear the exchange between the two characters – focus on their voices and the way that they speak to each other.

For this poem, imagine you are one of these two characters.

If you are the person making the proposal, how long have you been planning it? How important is it to you? How do you expect it to be received?

If you are the person receiving the proposal, were you expecting it? How do you feel about it? How will you respond?

Write a poem about the proposal, as your character, using the first person, 'I'. Address it to the other character, 'you.'

Take about twenty minutes.

Choice: A pilgrimage

Pilgrimage is a part of most faiths, but it can describe any journey that is made with a spiritual purpose, that is to say, has some kind of deep significance for the pilgrim.

Some people go on pilgrimages at transitional times in their lives, such as in the gap between school and university, or university and career, or at the end of their working life. They may set off in response to a diagnosis of terminal illness, or a recovery, or after a close bereavement.

Pilgrimages can take many months, or a few hours. I made one a few years ago to the island of Jura, because I wanted to read George Orwell's *1984* in the place where he wrote it. I felt that would be a way of deepening my understanding of both the author and his extraordinary novel.

Choose one of the following writing tasks on the theme of pilgrimage. Take about twenty minutes.

Memoir

Have you ever made a journey that wasn't primarily about getting from A to B, but had a conscious spiritual, religious or emotional significance for you? Write the story.

Fiction

Imagine a person setting off on a pilgrimage.

Where is their point of departure, and where is their journey's end?

Is someone making it with them, or are they alone?

Why are they making it? What are they seeking?

How will they make the journey, and how hard will it be for them, physically and emotionally?

Tell the story, in the first or third person, 'I' or 'he/she'.

Non-fiction

Write a travel article about a particular pilgrimage route, such as the Saints' Way or Santiago de Compostela.

If it's a route you have never taken, you may need to do some research before you start.

If it's one you have taken, you could write either an account of your personal experience, or let your piece take the form of tips and advice from someone who has been there.

Poetry

Imagine that you are making a pilgrimage. Where are you? Why are you making this pilgrimage? What do you want or need from it?

Use all your senses to conjure the scene. How are you feeling, in your body, in your clothes? How are your feet feeling, inside your shoes?

Have a rest. Sit Down for a while. Take out your notepad and pen.

Be there by the wayside in imagination, as you write your poem.

Memoir: Your birthday

When you were a child, how did your family celebrate your birthday? And when you were a teenager? Do any particular birthdays stand out in your mind?

How did you celebrate your birthdays throughout your adult life, right up to now? Do any particular ones stand out?

Either tell the story of one particular birthday you remember, including why you remember it so well, or write the history of all your birthdays.

Take about thirty minutes.

Fiction: This can't go on

Someone is having a tough time. What's the problem?

How long has the problem been going on?

Make some notes about the character and the situation, including anyone else who's involved.

Today is the day everything has come to a head. It's the last straw. Write a diary entry, as your main character, describing the events of the day. It may end with them recognising things can't go on the same way, but not knowing how to change the situation, or with them making a decision about what they're going to do about it.

Before you begin, feel your way into the character. Be in their room; be in their clothes. Hear their voice.

Picture their diary; imagine holding it in your hands. Is it big or small? Hardback or paperback? Plain or with a cover design?

Open it and notice the writing inside. Is it neat and small, or big and bold? Is it messy with lots of crossing out, or carefully tidy? Are there any drawings, or notes in the margins, or extra pieces of paper stuck in?

Use the conventions of diary making, starting with the date and time at the top, and write for twenty minutes.

Non-Fiction: A recipe for life

This exercise is a recipe, but not for food – it's a recipe for success in an area of life you feel you know about. For example, a recipe for a happy marriage/ amicable divorce/harmonious office/ perfect Sunday, for finding bargains or learning a language.

There are other areas you'll feel you've spectacularly failed in, and you could write about one of those instead – a recipe for a disastrous marriage, for example, or for getting scammed.

Write your piece following the convention for recipe writing, starting with 'You will need' or 'Ingredients' and continuing with 'Method.'

You can add some serving suggestions, tips or cautions at the end, and paint a picture in words of the finished dish.

Note: You're looking for life experience here, not something you can physically make, like an attractive item of knitwear or a raised flowerbed. That's too easy!

Poetry: The inner critic

Someone who came on a workshop once told me she pictured her inner critic as Stephen Fry being Jeeves, superior, supercilious and sarcastic. She imagined him coming in with a silver tray and white napkin over his arm, always ready to offer a polite but killer put-down.

For some people, the critic speaks with the voice of a parent or teacher from the past, or takes them by the throat, like a wild animal, and shakes them until all their creative joy has gone.

I picture my inner critic as a cross little goblin that occasionally turns up looking for trouble, and crouches in the corner, glaring at me.

Picture your inner critic. What kind of creature or person is it? Fully imagine what it looks like. Does it have a smell?

What does it say? Listen to its voice – not just the words, but the tone as well.

How does it make you feel?

How do you try to tackle or appease it?

Write a poem about an encounter with this creature/
person. Don't make it explicit that they represent your
inner critic.

Take about twenty minutes.

Choice: A visit

This task is about visiting a person rather than a place. Some examples might be visiting someone in hospital, or friends who live far away, or an elderly relative in their home, or your child at university.

Choose one of the following options, and write for twenty minutes.

Memoir

Jot down some occasions when you have visited someone, or someone has visited you. Go with whichever random memories come to you first, whether they're big occasions or nothing out of the ordinary.

Choose one, and write the story.

Fiction

Where is this visit taking place?

Who is visiting, and who is being visited?

What is the reason for the visit?

What does each of the characters hope it will be like – and what is it really like?

Choose which character you want to write as and tell the story, starting before the visitor arrives and ending after they have left.

How is your character changed by the visit?

Non-fiction

What are the golden rules for visitors? What are the rules for people receiving a visit?

Jot down some examples of visiting situations, such as visiting the in-laws, Christmas drinks with the neighbours or hosting an overseas student. Go with types of visit that you have personal experience of.

Write a serious or humorous piece of non-fiction giving advice to people visiting or being visited in a specific circumstance, such as 'Five things to remember if you want to get invited back' or 'Three golden rules for hospital visiting' or 'How not to embarrass your ten-year-old on parents' evening.'

Poetry

List some situations where people might visit each other, such as at times of illness, or celebration, or simply for a coffee and a chat.

Choose one.

Imagine it from the point of view of the person being visited. How do they feel about the visit? Picture the scene when the visitor arrives. Picture the visitor. What are they wearing? How do they seem?

Switch and be the visitor. How do you feel about the visit? Imagine yourself arriving; picture the scene; see the person or people you are visiting.

Decide which point of view you would like to explore the visit from – as the visitor or the one being visited – and write a poem.

Memoir: Best friends forever

Who is your best friend now? Who was your best friend in the past? You may have had several best friends at different stages in your life, or just one who's been there for you ever since primary school.

Choose one. What made or makes them your best friend? What were the experiences that cemented your friendship? Maybe you were the naughty kids at school, getting up to lots of mischief and fun, or maybe you were there for each other during difficult times, or both. Best friends are friends through thick and thin.

A while ago, I wrote this post for the children's blog, girlsheartbooks, explaining what made my childhood friend feel like a best friend forever.

What makes a bff?

When I was writing *How to get the friends you want, by Peony Pinker,* I got to thinking quite a bit about friends.

At school, I was one of those popular girls, always getting voted Form Rep and Sports Monitor and stuff like that, but as I got older I kind of dropped back. I felt more comfortable on the edge of the group, rather than right in the middle.

Then there was this really terrible year when some bad things happened in my life, and I stopped talking. I didn't know why; it wasn't a plan or anything. It was just as if my voice had suddenly disappeared. I lost all my friends then, because they thought I was being rude. Except one.

My bff Christine stayed friends with me, in a really clever way. She started writing to me. There was no internet or social media in those days, so we became pen friends, not talking, but writing long letters to each other.

She lives in Nottingham now, and I live in Cornwall, but she came down for the weekend a few weeks ago. It's a long, long time since we were at school, but I think sticking by me when I was having a tough time is what makes her a best friend forever.

Write a blog post about one of your best friends. Before you start, take some time to imagine your reader – what kind of person might read this particular blog? I imagined children reading mine.

Describe some experiences you shared with your friend that really cemented your friendship.

Finish with the situation now. Maybe you're no longer in touch, or maybe you see each other almost every day. What makes this friendship still feel precious to you?

All genres tip

Having a clear idea who you're writing for always helps you find not only the voice of the piece but also the content.

Fiction: Dreaming awake

Dreams and daydreams can be great starting points for stories, but what if none come along? How can you conjure a daydream at will?

One easy way is to start by visualising yourself in a familiar setting, and then introducing an unexpected element.

On a school visit, I might ask the children to visualise the end of the lesson, when the bell goes for playtime. I get them to imagine putting their books away, getting their coats on and going outside into the playground.

'So you run outside and… oh! What's this? There's some kind of vehicle in the middle of the playground – it might be a helicopter, or a tractor, or a spaceship…' Or I might suggest they imagine there's a building they've never noticed before in a far corner of the playground, a shed maybe, or a storage container.

I get them to walk right round the unexpected object – to touch it with their hand, to find a door.

They open the door. What's inside?

Whole stories spring up from this kind of visualisation, which is easy to get into because it starts somewhere we know. I often use the technique with adults too.

So close your eyes and picture yourself walking along the road from your house. Use all your senses, to really be there. What can you see and hear? What does the air smell like? What does the ground feel like beneath your feet? What time of day is it, and what time of year?

Notice all the familiar buildings, hedges, gardens, fences, fields – whatever is in your neighbourhood.

Now stop. What's this? A building you've never noticed before, set well back from the path.

Someone is watching you from a window. They beckon you in.

Let the adventure begin!

Write the story. Twenty minutes.

Non-Fiction: Unusual uses

Non-fiction isn't just about repeating things you know – it's also about expressing your own ideas. Exercise your inventiveness by thinking up some unusual uses for common objects. For example, a paper clip could also be used as a hairgrip, or you could fashion a hook from it and use it to pull gunk out of a plughole, or attach a little ornament and use it as a key ring. You could make a strong chain with lots of paperclips.

Dream up as many alternative uses as you can think of for these objects:

1. Uncooked rice

2. A park bench

3. A plastic bottle

4. A dead wasp

5. Old socks

Note: These can include real alternative uses not everyone might know about. For example, you can cut the bottom off a plastic bottle, remove the lid and use it to protect seedlings in the garden.

Another note: They don't all have to be possible or realistic. For example, old socks might make a sandwich filling no one would want to order.

Poetry: Happy

Lots of people go through a phase of writing poetry in their teenage years, to help them manage and express the complicated emotions they may be buffeted by, but then, as life levels out, they stop and never return to poetry again.

I think perhaps these early experiences can mean we associate writing poetry with feelings of angst, but poetry isn't only a place for exploring and expressing difficult feelings – it can range across all the emotions in the heart's library.

What makes you happy? Make a list. It will include activities, places and people. Some will make you feel happy for a moment, others for hours, and others throughout your whole life.

Write a poem about one of them. Rhyme it, if that feels right.

Enjoy the lift that writing about happy experience can bring.

Choice: The death of a pet

The death of a pet can be a devastating loss. It can carry all the same complications as the death of any human friend or family member – sadness, anger, anxiety, guilt and sometimes, depending on the circumstances, a sense of relief and closure.

Choose one of the following tasks, and write for about twenty minutes.

Memoir

Write this in the form of a letter, to a pet you once had that died. Tell them what they meant to you, and share some happy memories you have of them. Describe how their death affected you, and how you feel about it now.

Note: You may need to have some tissues handy.

Fiction

What kind of animal is the pet in your story? Who does it live with?

Jot down some character notes about the owner and/ or family.

How does the animal die? Is their death expected? Who is present at the death, or finds the body?

Write the story.

Non-fiction

Write an article about some aspect of the death of a pet, such as 'How to help your child when a beloved pet dies' or 'What happens when you take your pet to the vet for the final time?' or 'Why you might feel guilty when your pet dies – and how to handle it.'

Poetry

This is a farewell poem from beyond the grave, from a pet to the person or people who have lost them.

Before you start, fully imagine being the animal, living inside that little body, in its normal environment, with all its normal things.

Remember the period leading up to your death. Are you young or old? Full of life, or sick and weary? Loved or lonely? Happy or sad?

What is the pattern of your days and nights?

How did you die? Who was with you, or found your body?

Picture the person you are writing the poem to – a child, an elderly person, someone in a flat-share of friends?

What do you want them to know?

Write the poem.

Memoir: Playing

Drawing and writing with your non-dominant hand is a very effective way of remembering how it felt to be a young child, when you were just learning to control a pencil or pen.

With your non-dominant hand, draw a picture of yourself when you were little, playing somewhere you used to play – your bedroom, maybe, or in your childhood garden, at your grandparents' house, or in the playground at school.

Draw yourself, and also the background. Feel your way back to being the child you were. Take your time.

Still with your non-dominant hand, write a caption, describing what's happening in your picture. 'I am playing on my swing', 'Lulu and me are playing with the ball.'

Now, as the adult you are, reflecting back, write with your normal writing hand about how and where you used to play. Focus it down to a particular occasion if one springs to mind. 'But there was this one time...'

Take about ten minutes for the drawing and fifteen minutes for the writing.

Fiction: At the funfair

Picture a funfair you have been to, either recently or way back in the past. See it in its setting – a town centre car park, maybe, or a green field, or at the top of a beach. Remember as many of the rides and stalls as you can. Hear the sounds, see the bright lights and the people milling around.

All kinds of things can happen at a funfair. People can lose each other, find each other, fall in love. They may have mishaps or misunderstandings.

Imagine something happens at the funfair that you're picturing in your mind. Watch as the incident unfolds.

Write the story. Twenty minutes.

Fiction tip

People watching is a great skill to develop if you want to write fiction. Use occasions when you are alone in a crowd – in a café, perhaps, or an art gallery, on a train or at the beach – to notice the people around you and imagine where they live and what's going on in their life.

Non-Fiction: Your own free-range forays

Write your own set of free-range forays – you know how this goes now! Devise one writing task in each genre: memoir, fiction, non-fiction and poetry.

Start straight in with some brainstorming lists – just any random ideas that come to you, off the top of your head. Chocolate, office politics, favourite aunts and uncles, burger chains, hamsters, springtime…

Decide which one you're going with for each of the four genres and make some notes. Take about five minutes for this part.

Write a section for each one, giving it a title and including as many writing instructions as you like. Some of mine offer step-by-step instructions but others give barely any guidance at all. Add some writing tips if you can think of any. Take about twenty-five minutes.

Note: If you like an extra challenge, you could just choose one topic from your list and write four different forays on the same theme, as I have in my 'Choice' sections.

Another note: If you're in a writing group, you could have a session where each person brings a free-range writing task they've devised for everyone to try.

Poetry: A family photo

Find an old family photo with at least two people in it. Study it closely. Note what the people are wearing. What do their clothes say about them?

How closely are they standing to each other? What does their body language say about the relationship/s between them, at the moment the photo was taken?

What do you notice about the background and setting? How do the people in the photo feel about being there?

Write a poem describing what you see in the photo. Take about thirty minutes. If you finish early, fill the rest of the time trying out different versions.

Poetry tip

A poem is so short that you can easily experiment with different drafts, playing around with words, images, ideas and the way the poem is laid out on the page.

Don't be afraid to play!

Choice: Poison

Poison, in both its literal and metaphorical sense, is a gift of a subject for writers in all genres.

What kind of writing do you fancy doing right now? Take your pick!

Memoir

When I was about five, my siblings and I feasted on the berries that had fallen from the tree in our garden, and we got very sick.

When I was a young adult, fear of one individual tipped over into full-blown panic attacks, and I fantasised about sending them a poisoned present through the post, like a real life Agatha Christie villain.

My sister poisoned herself with painkillers, and nearly died.

Once in my life, I had such bad food poisoning, I thought I was going to die.

Have you ever had a brush with poison, or has somebody close to you?

Tell the story. Twenty minutes.

Fiction

This story is about a toxic relationship, rather than a literal poisoning.

Whose health and happiness is being undermined by someone else?

Who do they need to get away from?

What makes them realise they have to?

How do they try to break away?

Do they succeed or fail?

Write the story. Twenty minutes.

Non-fiction

What do you know about poisons? For example, do you know the most hazardous products for toddlers that are commonly found in the home? Or the most toxic plants in a garden? Or how to tell edible fungi from poisonous ones?

Decide on your topic, and write some notes. Do a bit of research, checking your facts and adding to them. Take fifteen minutes for this part.

Write an article. Take another fifteen minutes.

Poetry

Write a gleeful poem about poisons. You could be a witch, mixing a potion, adding all kinds of disgusting ingredients, or a child playing a game of pretend. You could be yourself, enjoying a wicked fantasy.

What's in your potion? What effect will it have? Not all poisonings result in death, but they all have unwanted results. Be bad! Be very bad, and enjoy it!

This is the perfect opportunity for a good strong pattern of rhythm and rhyme.

Take as long as you like – I wouldn't want to cross you!

Memoir: Work

When you were still at school, did you have a Saturday job? If you went to college, did you do paid work in the evenings or vacations? What was your first full-time job?

Jot down a list of all the jobs you've ever had.

What was your childhood ambition? Have you fulfilled it, or grown out of it – or do you still hold it in your heart?

Write an overview of your working life, then focus in on one particular period, or one job, and tell the story.

Take twenty minutes.

Fiction: Write what you know

What have been the most important, joyful or challenging experiences you've been through? Jot down some ideas.

Choose one. Really feel your way into it, and then tell the story – take ten minutes.

Now create a character who will live through the same experience. Make them a different gender from you and, if possible, a different age. Give them a different social and geographical situation.

Tell the story of this character living through the same significant experience as you have. Keep the emotional essence and make it just as significant for them.

Take twenty minutes.

Fiction tip

All fiction is emotionally autobiographical, whether we're aware of it or not, and a lot of fiction writers use this technique quite deliberately in order to explore their own lived experiences because it feel less exposing that writing memoir.

Non-Fiction: About the author

Authors have to write 'About the author' paragraphs for different books and projects, but life is large, and a paragraph is small, so what goes in has to be adapted according to the specific publication.

For example, in your 'About the author' for an article on looking after rescue dogs, the fact you've got a poodle called Poppy might be the most relevant thing to include and some bigger ticket items like your career and qualifications wouldn't need to feature at all.

In your 'About the author' paragraph for your detective novel, you'd certainly mention your twenty years' working as a pathologist, but your readers won't be interested in your dog!

Imagine you are about to publish four different pieces of writing:

1. A memoir of your childhood.

2. A novel set in a place you've lived in – the East End of London/the Scottish Highlands/suburban Manchester/ wherever.

3. An article about your favourite holiday destination for a travel magazine.

4. Your winning entry in a poetry competition.

Write a different 'About the author' paragraph for each of them. Like most short pieces, this will probably involve a lot of crossing out and rewriting, before you feel you've nailed it.

Take about seven minutes for each.

Poetry: Bed

Tracy Emin's artwork, 'My Bed', caused a furore when it was shortlisted for the Turner Prize in 1999, but it's an image that tells a vivid and memorable story.

A bed is a liminal space, between sleeping and waking, and maybe between people, moving in and out of each other, just as they move in and out of waking life and the dream.

What is the state of your bed right now? Is it made, or unmade? What are the fabrics, colours and condition of your linen? What stains or smells cling to the sheets?

Look all around your bed – what's on your bedside table? What's lying on the floor?

Make a poem that creates a picture of your bed, exactly as it is right now. Describe it in detail, and just stick to describing it – let the image tell the story of your life right now.

Call your poem, 'My Bed.'

Keep going until your poem feels finished.

Choice: Home

Home is more than bricks and mortar; it's more than family, or the people who share your living space. Home is an archetypal idea of comfort and safety. Home is where we belong.

Memoir

Whatever is going on in my world – joyful or painful – I always come home to my writing. I ground myself in my journal, and also in books, blogs, articles and workshops.

What is your 'home'? Where do you feel completely at ease with yourself and the world? You may have more than one 'home' – mine will include my family, friends and a few familiar places, as well as my writing.

The activities, people and places that give you this sense of belonging may change in the course of your life. Before I was a writer, I would come home to painting and drawing whenever I felt restless or unsettled. I used to feel socially at home in a big group of families, but that group has since dispersed, so I have other friendship groups I come home to now.

Think about the activities, people and places that are and have been nurturing to you in your life. Write whatever comes for twenty minutes.

Fiction

Someone has lost their home. Maybe they have been evicted, or have separated from their partner, or run away, or left the army and they've got nowhere to go.

Write some character notes – their name, age and appearance. How have they got into this situation? How have they tried to cope with it? Where will they sleep tonight?

Twenty minutes' writing is too short to solve all their problems, so in this story, give your protagonist just a moment of comfort and hope, when they feel connected to the world again, less alienated and alone.

Non-fiction

Write a magazine article about a particular lifestyle, under the title, 'When... is your home.' For example, 'When a University Hall of Residence is Your Home', 'When a Mansion in Surrey is Your Home', 'When a Cabin in the Woods is Your Home.'

Describe what characterises that kind of living. Make up some short 'real life' case studies, and put their stories in boxes, to illustrate your piece with examples.

Take thirty minutes.

Poetry

In his poem, *The Peace of Wild Things*, Wendell Berry describes where he goes when he feels anxious and unsafe in the world. If you don't know the poem, you might like to start by reading it online.

What about you? Where do you go to when you need to lose yourself and feel at one with life? Begin your poem, as Berry does, 'When...' When you feel what? What thoughts and fears can unsettle you?

What places, activities or people can ground you again? How does it feel, coming home to them?

Keep your poem loose and free, without any regular pattern of rhythm and rhyme. Enjoy the movement it brings, from a sense of alienation to feeling connected again.

Stories and memoir –
some general pointers

There are specific tips and suggestions included in most of the tasks, but here are some general pointers for writing stories, whether they're dreamed up in your imagination or remembered from your past.

Don't try to hold all these considerations in your mind when you start writing. They're just here for reference. The interest is the story, and stories come out all on their own if you let them, like dreams.

<u>Action</u>

Something has to happen! When you're writing stories, it can help to think of them like anecdotes you might tell in conversation, or scenes in a movie. Otherwise, it's easy to lose focus and drift into just describing the thoughts, emotions and inner lives of your characters or writing long descriptions of the settings, and losing the narrative thrust.

Most stories have the same basic structure: somebody wants something, they try to get it, they meet with opposition, which may be from other people, the environment or their own inner conflicts, and the result is they either succeed or fail.

That structure is developed over many scenes in a novel, and it's also the basic form of each scene within the novel and the kind of short pieces you're writing in these free-range forays.

Characters

Somebody wants something – so who? You need to know your protagonist (main character) and, if there is one, your antagonist (the one who tries to thwart him/her).

You need to know much more about them than you're going to include in the story because, if you don't know them, you won't know how they'll act and react in the particular circumstances of this scene.

That's why most of the fiction forays in this book start with making some character notes; if you can't get started or keep going with a story, the solution is often to find out more about your main characters.

Ask them questions, in the way you might ask someone in real life random things just to get to know them better. What's your earliest memory? What do you think of your boss? Where are you going for your holidays?

What the reader sees in the story is the tip of the iceberg; the writer has to also know what lies beneath.

Beginnings and endings

Don't worry about getting the beginning right – just get started. Beginnings almost always need redrafting because, when you start writing, you can't be entirely sure how things will turn out.

Once you know the whole story, you can rework the beginning, like adjusting a way marker once you've pinpointed the exact destination.

Check where the action actually starts, where the story 'catches.' You can often cut the first few lines or even paragraphs, which were just you writing your way in.

Once you know the whole story, you'll also have a much better idea of the main character, and the kind of story it is, so you can go back to the beginning and adjust the voice and style.

The beginning and ending should work together, bringing the action full circle, so that the reader notices the journey of the story – what did the character want at the outset, did they succeed or fail?

Often, you can put little echoes in, perhaps picking up, towards the ending, a detail in the scenery that you mentioned in the beginning, to enhance that sense of a journey by reminding the reader of how it began.

<u>Style</u>

A lot of new writers worry about their writing style, because they may have learnt in school that there's a right and wrong way to write, or a good and bad way.

The right and good way to write is whatever way springs naturally from you.

In the first instance write as you would speak. Imagine you're telling the story in conversation, and take dictation from your mind. That's how to find and develop your own voice.

If you find yourself trying to write well, you're probably overwriting. You don't need fancy words or constructions unless, of course, that's what floats your boat, in which case it will be part of your natural voice.

You can develop your voice through reading because, once you start writing, you notice what other writers do that you don't do, and what you do that they don't, which helps you hear your own voice. You can also experiment with techniques they use, to see if they will work and sound authentic for you.

Having said that, there are a few recommendations I could make. Most writers try to avoid using too many adverbs (words that add to the sense of the verb, and usually end –ly). It's more dynamic to use strong verbs instead. For example, 'she followed him reluctantly' could be 'she traipsed after him.' 'He took hold of her arm roughly' could be 'He grabbed her by the arm.'

Abstract nouns also tend to slow things up, so replace them with more active constructs where you can. For example, 'He was full of elation' could be 'He wanted to jump for joy'; 'She was overcome by guilt' could be 'She couldn't look him in the eye.'

Finally, when you're writing dialogue, stick to 'said.' Don't bother with 'asked' or 'replied', be sparing with words like 'whispered' or 'screeched' and avoid unusual ones such as 'opined' and 'remonstrated' like the plague.

Sticking to 'said' in dialogue is the one occasion when it doesn't matter how much you repeat the same word in a passage of prose. Readers barely notice it, so it doesn't distract them from just listening to what the characters are saying.

You don't always need to specify who's speaking if it's obvious in the context, especially when the conversation is between just two characters. You can also occasionally indicate who's speaking by linking their words to actions. For example:

'What shall I say?' said Tessa, rummaging in her bag for her phone.

'What shall I say?' Tessa rummaged in her bag for her phone.

Narrative voice

If you're telling a story from the point of view of the protagonist, either in the third person 'he/she' or the first person 'I', then the voice you're looking for is their voice. Write how they would speak.

What kind of thing would they notice or care about? What aspects of the action matter to them, and what's their attitude towards other people and the situation that's unfolding?

What age are they? Where did they grow up, geographically? What kind of social culture did they grow up in? All these things will affect how they talk and see the world.

Getting the voice right is another reason why you really need to know your protagonist well.

Settings

When you're imagining the places where the action is unfolding, use all your senses. Be your character, in that place, and notice what you can see and hear, the smell of the air, how the ground feels beneath your feet.

What time of day is it? What time of year?

Using your senses is how to ground yourself in an imaginary setting; if you also give some of this information in your writing, your reader can see, touch, hear, smell and fully imagine the setting too.

Don't overdo it, of course. Too much description will slow the story down. You just need enough to help the reader to picture in their mind what you are picturing in yours.

Emotions

Emotions are physical; we feel them in our bodies. So when you're imagining being your protagonist, feeling what they're feeling emotionally, notice where that is in your body.

If you describe your characters' emotions by describing how they feel in their body – 'her heart melted', 'his pulse quickened', 'she caught her breath', 'he slumped down in his chair' – your reader will feel it in their body too.

Describing emotions through body language, rather than telling the reader what your characters are feeling is part of show-don't-tell.

Show-don't-tell

Actions speak louder than words. You don't have to say that a character is, for example, very polite if you show it in the way they behave. You don't have to spell out how they feel if you show it in the bodily sensations they're experiencing.

If you've spelt it out in places in your first draft, often as a kind of reminder to yourself, you can usually cut those bits as the characters become more established in your mind, and take on a life of their own.

Show-don't-tell is about focusing on action – which brings me back round to the beginning of this chapter. (Following my own advice on beginnings and endings!)

I suggested at the beginning of this chapter that you don't try to hold all these considerations in your mind before you start writing, but just focus on the story you want to tell.

Story making is a natural process – it's how the human mind organises and understands experience. Therefore the more you write the more you'll notice that you are already instinctively incorporating most of these ideas anyway.

Non-fiction — why it's not out of bounds

There are two common misconceptions about writing non-fiction: firstly, that it doesn't require the same level of inspiration and craft as writing fiction, because it's basically just a list of facts, and secondly, that you have to be an expert in a subject before you can write non-fiction about it.

It's not just a list of facts!

There are facts and then there's how you tell them, and non-fiction has a voice, just like fiction. What's your angle? Most of my children's self-help books are funny, and I'm friendly and present as the narrator. I like to be present in my adult non-fiction too. I hope it feels like a conversation.

But that's my choice. You might prefer not to use a personal voice or give your non-fiction pieces something of your personality. In my educational books, I tend to stay out of it, so you won't see 'I' or 'me' at all. But I still present the facts in a variety of different ways.

I love that there are choices about the form you choose, such as 'how to' instructions or menus, numbered lists, factual recounts, Q and A pieces, essays and arguments. Just as much as fiction, the pleasure of writing non-fiction is that it's playful. Facts and ideas might be a function of the rational mind, but how we write about them begins, as Jung says, with the play instinct. We play with them, like a child stringing beads.

To add to the creative excitement, non-fiction has some lovely special features that fiction doesn't have. You can add text boxes and bullet-points, headings and subheadings, maps and diagrams, illustrations – all kinds of ways of embellishing and adding interest to your main text.

Non-fiction has structure just like fiction, too. It needs a beginning, middle and end, and they work in a similar way. The beginning introduces the subject, and the ending returns to the beginning by summarising what has happened in between. For example, I introduced this chapter by saying there are two common misconceptions about writing non-fiction, now I'm exploring what they are, and in a minute I'll end the chapter by reminding you where we started at the beginning, before rounding it off.

There's no need to be an expert.

The level of expertise you need depends upon who you're writing for, and the vast majority of non-fiction out there is written for the general reader rather than professionals and academics.

You can write from what you know, in any field you like, so long as you check your facts and support your opinions with evidence. I've written books for primary age children on physics, history, geography – all sorts of things I only have a basic understanding in – because although I don't have any special training, I certainly have more understanding than a six year-old, and can look up what I don't already know when I'm writing for older children.

Magazine articles are usually not specialised either. If you've got a garden, you can write about it. If you remember the 1980s, you can write about that. If you've had a great day out... you know what to do!

The key to writing great non-fiction is to write about what interests you. As in all kinds of writing, follow your heart.

Everyone has knowledge and experience, and that means everyone can write non-fiction. Everyone can enjoy writing it too because, far from being just a list of facts, it's as much a creative adventure as every other kind of writing.

The joy of poetry — there are no rules!

Sometimes, people are put off writing poetry because they feel they don't know how to do it properly. I think this comes from the way we learn to read and write poems at school, where the emphasis is often on forms and structures, rhyme schemes and scansion, and where symbolic meanings may be reduced to interpretations that leave children feeling confused.

As with most creative subjects on the school curriculum, we complicate something that should be natural and instinctive by loading it prematurely with theories and analysis.

Coming back to writing poetry as an adult can be a joy and revelation because, these days, there really are no rules. You can use a traditional form if you want to, but you don't have to. You don't even need to know what traditional forms such as sonnets and sestinas are.

So if a poem doesn't have to rhyme or scan, what makes it a poem?

What is a poem?

A poem is just a short piece of writing that has a visual aspect in the way it's laid out on the page. Because of its short scope, the musicality and flow of the language is very noticeable so, although it need not have an overall rhyming structure, there may be internal rhythms and rhymes, alliterations (using words with the same initial consonants), assonances (words with the same internal vowel sounds), repetitions – every kind of sound play you can create with words.

Again, because of its scope, a poem can make you feel the symbolic power of ordinary objects. You can use metaphors and similes if you like, and make the connections explicit –'the blue bird of happiness', 'as happy as a blue bird flying high up in the sky...' But simply describing something within the close focus of a poem will set up resonances for you and your reader.

You don't need to start with an idea of what you want your poem to mean – in fact, that puts an automatic limit on its potential to surprise and delight you. You don't need to spell it out for your reader either; let them make their own discoveries too.

Denise Levertov has written about this mysterious exchange between poem, poet and reader in her wonderful poem, *The Secret*. Definitely worth a read.

<u>Rhyming or non-rhyming?</u>

I personally prefer non-rhyming poetry, both as a reader and a writer. Partly, that's because it feels more contemporary to me, but I also find fixed forms draw attention to themselves and distract attention from the subject.

Keeping it free means you can focus fully on the objects, themes and narratives in your poem and, through that focus, begin to feel the symbolic resonance they carry.

Having said that, rhyming structures can work well – an example for me would be Kate Light's poem, *There Comes The Strangest Moment* – and I'd always consider using rhyming verse for humorous or narrative poems.

Rhyming verse can be more effective for performance poetry, where you aren't offering a lingering chance to ponder and of course, if you're writing a rap you're going to need a strong rhythm and rhyme.

When it comes to writing poetry, trust your instincts. Unhook your analytical brain. Feel the movement of your ideas, and the sound of your words. Nudge and shuffle them; arrange them in different ways, until your poem looks and sounds pleasing to you.

You can even mess about with punctuation and sentence structure. It's the ultimate free-range writing!

How to set up a free-range writing group

A writing group is a unique social situation, where people who may not know each other outside the group come together to explore and share glimpses of their inner lives.

Some writing groups focus on critiquing work for each other, with a view to possible publication, but free-range writing isn't primarily about the craft; it's about the adventure. It's about exploring every area of life, and bringing what you find inside you out onto the page.

What you discover and share in a free-range writing group isn't just the stories and themes of your imagination in fiction, but stories from your real life too, in memoir. You share your knowledge and ideas in non-fiction and, in poetry, the sensibility of your soul.

When people are sharing their writing in my groups, I often think of elders sitting under a tree at the end of the day, celebrating and reflecting upon the extraordinary richness of ordinary life.

It may sound as if a free-range writing group won't help you to write better, but the surprising thing is, it will. This is the practice school of writing, learning from doing, rather than from theory, and learning from each other.

When you share what you've written, you hear its qualities reflected back to you in other people's responses, and when you hear what other people have written, you see what they do that you don't, and get ideas for improving your own writing.

So how do you go about creating a free-range writing group?

You will need:

- A group! Two or three people are enough to get started, because it will grow; five to six is ideal, eight is your absolute max. Maybe you already have a couple of writing friends but, if not, you could put an ad in a local publication or website and set up an inaugural meeting.

- A venue. In the first instance, the back room of a pub or café could be good, as there will be refreshments available, but the space does need to be quiet and private. Community halls and libraries sometimes have rooms you can hire for a small fee, and it might be worth checking out your local bookshop too. If it's just you and a few friends in the first instance, you could just meet up in each other's homes.

- A time. You need a two-hour session ideally, and you'll have to decide how often you're going to meet. Most writing groups I've visited seem to meet once a month but you can always adjust that depending on your particular group's preferences. Bear in mind that meeting in the evening will work for more people than daytime or weekends, when many have work and family commitments.

Once you've found your group, chosen a venue and set a time, then you're good to go. Here's how to organise your sessions.

A free-range writing session.

First, set some rules. This is important, because boundaries create a sense of safety. Here are mine:

1. Confidentiality. We may share things with each other in the group that we wouldn't necessarily want to share with the world.

2. Safety. I ask people to keep themselves safe by not writing about big emotional issues they're currently struggling with, because the focus of my groups is creative rather than therapeutic.

3. No negative criticism – of other people's work, or

of your own. I especially don't like it when people say, 'I'll read it, but it's not very good.' It's a first draft – it's not supposed to be good! When we share something we've only just written, we're telling our stories, and we're listening for what engages, moves and intrigues us in other people's.

When you've given a reminder of the rules, choose a free-range foray, set a timer and start writing. Stick to the suggested writing time. It doesn't matter if you haven't all finished when the time's up; you can still share what you've written, and then describe how you are planning to finish the piece.

If anyone finishes early, there will always be redrafting they could do until the time is up. It's important not to disturb the silent concentration of the writing period, and most people naturally respect that but, if someone doesn't, rather than put them on the spot right there and then, you might want to start the next session with a general reminder.

When you've all finished writing, take a few minutes to read back over what you've written and give it a title.

Now you come to the part many writers enjoy the most – the sharing. As this is one of the most pleasurable and insightful aspects of writing in a group, encourage everyone to read, or at least to share something.

If someone doesn't want to read their whole piece, they might be happy to read a section of it and describe the rest, or they might be willing to describe how the experience of writing was for them, or talk about the ideas they've had for the task. Ideally, you want to hear everyone's voice in every session, although no one should feel obliged to share more than they want to.

Because free-range writing forays are so varied, different people will be playing to their strengths or writing outside their comfort zone in different sessions, so everyone gets the chance to feel the fear and do it anyway, both with the writing and the sharing.

Try to finish the session at the end of your two hours, because it can be easy to overrun. If you all know the finish time, you'll naturally pace yourselves and divide the sharing time equally between you, not spending too long chatting about one person's writing.

The free-range forays are perfect for groups because 20-30 minutes' writing time produces fairly short pieces of written work, and that means there's time for everyone to read theirs if they want to. One foray will work perfectly for groups of up to eight. If your group is only three or four, you may have time to do two forays in each session.

Other kinds of writing group

You can select particular writing forays from this book to set up a poetry group, say, or a fiction writing group, by just using the poetry or fiction tasks and following the same format for sessions.

If you're already in a writing group, you might try a few free-range forays and see how it feels to divert from your usual format and genre for part or all of your session.

Creativity is dynamic. It's good to shake things up from time to time!

The 75 forays tick list

1. Memoir: The history of your writing

2. Fiction: The stranger on the bridge

3. Non-Fiction: How to...

4. Poetry: You are...

5. Choice: A day out

6. Memoir: I remember

7. Fiction: Feeling bad, feeling better

8. Non-Fiction: An interview with yourself

9. Poetry: I am... I once... I will...

10. Choice: The lie

11. Memoir: But one particular day...

12. Fiction: Writing the intense moment

13. Non-Fiction: Life's lessons

14. Poetry: Ways to get rich

15. Choice: Three words

16. Memoir: Dear Diary

17. Fiction: The put-down

18. Non-Fiction: Valentine's Day Q and A

19. Poetry: Similes, fresh and funny

20. Choice: A conversation

21. Memoir: Didn't we have a lovely time?

22. Fiction: Out in the cold

23. Non-Fiction: Top tips

24. Poetry: Don't tell me

25. Choice: Fire

26. Memoir: The history of shoes in your life

27. Fiction: I am writing to complain...

28. Non-Fiction: A review

29. Poetry: A madeleine

30. Choice: Looking for love

31. Memoir: Mother

32. Fiction: Better than they thought

33. Non-Fiction: I love...

34. Poetry: Waking up

35. Choice: An interview

36. Memoir: Your future self

37. Fiction: Feel the feelings

38. Non-Fiction: Facts

39. Poetry: The poetry persona

40. Choice: A meal

41. Memoir: Father

42. Fiction: Running

43. Non-Fiction: Selling

44. Poetry: The best thing

45. Choice: Physical illness

46. Memoir: All your teachers

47. Fiction: Something happened on the way to...

48. Non-Fiction: The problem with...

49. Poetry: Just this

50. Choice: Gifts

51. Memoir: The view from your window

52. Fiction: A life in five days

53. Non-Fiction: The best of times, the worst of times

54. Poetry: The proposal

55. Choice: A pilgrimage

56. Memoir: Your birthday

57. Fiction: This can't go on

58. Non-Fiction: A recipe for life

59. Poetry: The inner critic

60. Choice: A visit

61. Memoir: Best friends forever

62. Fiction: Dreaming awake

63. Non-Fiction: Unusual uses

64. Poetry: Happy

65. Choice: The death of a pet

66. Memoir: Playing

67. Fiction: At the funfair

68. Non-Fiction: Your own free-range forays

69. Poetry: A family photo

70. Choice: Poison

71. Memoir: Work

72. Fiction: Write what you know

73. Non-Fiction: About the author

74. Poetry: Bed

75. Choice: Home

Final word

This book could not have been written without all the wonderful teachers whose workshops I have attended and all the many and various writers who have attended mine.

I'd like to thank especially my five brilliant beta readers: Fiona Saint, Liz Berg, Kim Brown, Debs Casey and Jenny Cole. Their thoughtful and constructive feedback on the manuscript of this book helped me enormously to craft and complete it.

If you have enjoyed reading it, please

- Let me know. (Writing emails is a fine non-fiction foray).

- Post a review. (So is writing reviews).

- Keep writing!

Many thanks

Jenny Alexander

Ps If you haven't already read it, you can find some further forays in the ebook taster, *A Little Bit of Free-Range Writing: 10 Forays For The Wild Writer's Soul.*

About the author

Jenny Alexander's free-range writing career began in 1995. Her books for children include novels, fiction series, chapter books, educational fiction and non-fiction, self-help books and interactive CDRoms. For adults, she has written four non-fiction books, a dozen articles for mainstream magazines, several prize-winning poems and an Apple app, *Get Writing!*

Besides writing for publication, Jenny blogs at www.writinginthehouseofdreams.com She's been writing journals about all sorts of things ever since she was in primary school.

More resources for writers by Jenny Alexander

Books

Happy Writing: Beat Your Blocks, Be Published and Find Your Flow

Every writer is different and so is every block – there's no one-size-fits-all solution. Whether you're an established author or a complete beginner, this book will help you identify what's holding you back whenever you feel stuck and develop strategies for dealing with it.

A wonderful book... wise and inspirational. Linda Newbery, Costa Prize Winner

Writing in the House of Dreams: Unlock the Power of Your Unconscious Mind

Creative ideas and dreams spring naturally from the unconscious but the rational mind can get in the way. For writers, it's the inner critic and for dreamers, the need to analyse and interpret. The skills you need in order to bypass these blocks are the same for writers and dreamers, and this guide will help you understand and master them.

An astonishing book. I don't think I've read another like it. Susan Price, Carnegie Medal Winner

Apple app

Get Writing!

Writing whatever comes into your head for twenty minutes every day is a tried and tested way to bust through writer's block, but some people find it too unfocused. This app gives you twenty-eight short writing tasks that gradually build up to a finished story, from planning to redrafting, in twenty minutes a day.

Workshops

Jenny teaches workshops on every aspect of writing. Find out more at www.jennyalexander.co.uk where you can also sign up for her newsletter.

.

Lightning Source UK Ltd.
Milton Keynes UK
UKHW010624050821
388357UK00002B/123